D1649348

All the Ideas

LIVING IN MY HEAD

*One Guy's Musings
About Truth*

DON EVERTS

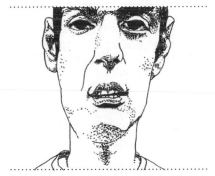

IVP Books

An imprint of InterVarsity Press
Downers Grove, Illinois

InterVarsity Press
P.O. Box 1400, Downers Grove, IL 60515-1426
World Wide Web: www.ivpress.com
E-mail: email@ivpress.com

InterVarsity Press® is the book-publishing division of InterVarsity Christian Fellowship/USA®, a student movement active on campus at hundreds of universities, colleges and schools of nursing in the United States of America, and a member movement of the International Fellowship of Evangelical Students. For information about local and regional activities, write Public Relations Dept., InterVarsity Christian Fellowship/USA, 6400 Schroeder Rd., P.O. Box 7895, Madison, WI 53707-7895, or visit the IVCF website at <www.intervarsity.org>.

All Scripture quotations, unless otherwise indicated, are taken from the Holy Bible, Today's New International Version™ Copyright © 2001 by International Bible Society. All rights reserved.

Illustrations and design by Matt Smith

ISBN 978-0-8308-3611-6

Printed in the United States of America ∞

Library of Congress Cataloging-in-Publication Data

Everts, Don, 1971-
   All the ideas living in my head: one guy's musings about truth/
Don Everts.
     p. cm.—(One guy's head)
   Includes bibliographical references.
   ISBN-13: 978-0-8308-3611-6 (pbk.: alk. paper)
   1. Thought and thinking—Religious
aspects—Christianity—Miscellanea. 2. Truth—Religious
aspects—Christianity—Miscellanea. I. Title.
BV4598.4.E94 2007
230—dc22

163603960   2007031455

P	15	14	13	12	11	10	9	8	7	6	5	4	3	2	1
Y	19	18	17	16	15	14	13	12	11	10	09	08	07		

Contents

INTRODUCTION:
MY HEAD

This is not so much a book about how to think as it is a book about how I think. And that's an important distinction.

I am not writing as a professional philosopher, cognitive theorist or well-versed psychologist. If I were, I would probably be writing a book about how to think. But as I said, I'm not doing that.

I am writing as a guy. A guy who thinks. And therefore I am writing about *how I think*. In that sense this little book is adequately described as confessional. I am writing about all the ideas that live up in my head and how those ideas get in there and how they behave once there.

I'll go more into my journey toward writing such an odd book in chapter one. But for now I will say that I am trying to write as a guy who is being honest (and honestly descriptive) about how he thinks. My sincere hope is that such honesty—such potentially embarrassing honesty—will be of some sort of actual, tangible service to you, the reader.

My goal, after all, is not to provide some sort of cerebral flashing or intellectual peep show. It's really not. I want to encourage more relaxed conversations and honest self-reflection. I want to litter this world with fresh language. And I hope that my own confession will help us all (myself included) practice the exquisite, everyday, joyful art of thinking more and more all the time.

Chapter 1

THINKING ABOUT THINKING ABOUT THINKING

Since I'm inviting you on a tour of my brain, and since you apparently want to take that tour, I figured I'd start you out with a little history. Consider this chapter the short and sweet welcome speech at the visitor's center at the beginning of the tour.

For starters, I have been thinking nearly all my life. No promises or claims about the quality of that thinking. I'd rather not get into that. Just regular thinking, I imagine.

It was only in the last several years that I began thinking *about* my thinking. I started doing that because I kept running into people who described thinking in ways that didn't make complete sense to me. Their words and metaphors for thinking made me feel as if maybe I wasn't going about my thinking exactly right.

THE MODERN CAMP

I'd talk to some folks (a bit older usually) who

talked about the project of thinking as if it were an
exact science. They'd talk about evidence and truth
and logic and propositions, and they said stuff like
clearly and *therefore* and *inherent contradictions* a lot.
They made it seem as if thinking was like being a
scientist. Or worse, a mathematician. They made it
seem as if this human thinking endeavor was exact-
ing and measured. When they were talking about
truth or the "quest for truth" (which incidentally is
a much too exciting title for the process they'd
then go on to describe), it all felt like my brain was
in a big equation in algebra.

Remember those equations? Where you'd have to
be sure to follow the rules? Where everything on the
left side of the equals sign had to match up with the
other side? And if you wanted to do something simple like subtract three from the left side, you sure as
heck had better be subtracting it from the other side
as well? All in a quest to isolate the variable.

Folks talked about thinking like that. Everything
seemed to make perfect sense to them. It was all
just a matter of deducing, calculating, figuring out
the variable—which was truth, I imagine. Or Truth,
rather. (They talked about truth such that you felt
guilty if you forgot to capitalize it.)

Problem was, it just didn't feel like that in my
head. A lot of the ideas rolling around in my head
wouldn't sit still like a nice little variable and let me
work the whole thing out. Also, there were some

ideas up there that other people would show me again and again on the chalkboard how they should just be subtracted right out. And yet it wasn't quite that simple. Those ideas would stay on for the ride somehow.

So I never quite felt at home in that set of words and metaphors for talking about truth and thinking. If you consider that "modern" thinking, I don't think I'm all that modern. Stuff's just not quite so sequential up in my head (as you'll soon see). And to be honest, this nonmathematical nature of my thinking didn't really bother me. The ideas running around in my head didn't seem much like disembodied propositions. And my thinking wasn't all that ordered. Not as ordered as these modern folks made it seem thinking should feel like, anyway.

So I pulled up my tent and walked out of that modern camp. Either these people weren't quite describing things right or my thinking was really wrong.

THE POSTMODERN CAMP

Well, I soon found welcome in a new camp. "Postmodern" was the name put up on the banner at the entrance to the camp, though I can't say I've ever taken to the name. At first I felt much more comfortable in this new camp. In *this* camp folks would make fun of words like *truth* and *logic* and *propositions*. So I joined right in. It was great making fun of all those old scientist types, and with my goatee and messy hair, I seemed to fit right in at this new camp.

But then things started getting a little funny there too. You see, after all the making fun of the old-timers, there'd be this awkward silence in camp. We all knew we didn't fit in back at the other camp (our brains didn't work *that* way), but we weren't really sure what new words to start using to talk about the thinking going on upstairs. Sure, truth wasn't like a specimen in a petri dish—we sure knew that! But . . . well, what *was* it like?

And so folks drank their coffee and listened to loud music and started talking about our heads and what was really going on up there and what this thinking was really all about. The only problem was that the new words the camp came up with still didn't quite sit right with me. Not a perfect fit, anyway. Instead of being on a Calculated Quest for Truth, we were on Windy Pathways of Truth. Not pathways *to* truth, mind you. Truth wasn't a destination; it was the path, the going along, you see.

Experience and *resonance* and *perspective* and *journey* became the holy words. At first it bugged me that people weren't talking about my head much at all. It was the heart and the soul and the body get-

ting the airtime. So I wasn't sure if all that stuff going on upstairs was supposed to be going on, if it
was valid or if (gulp) I really was supposed to be
back in that modern camp. I mean, I felt it all going
on up there. Like I said, I have been thinking nearly
all my life. So when these goateed friends of mine
would talk about the free-form, heart-soul-body-
embraced journeys of experience, I felt a little out
of place.

It's not that I didn't have a sense of my heart and
my soul and my body. I did. But I still felt my head
go right on thinking. I wasn't sure exactly what was
going on up there, but I felt a sort of . . . *order* to it
that didn't fit into the experiential metaphors. It
wasn't order like you'd find in an algebra class, but
it was definitely order of some kind. Which made
me feel just as unsettled and awkward in this new
camp as in the one I had left.

I felt like a man without a home. Just too unsci-
entific for the modern camp and just too ordered
to make for a decent postmodern (my goatee and
cynicism notwithstanding).

A MAN WITHOUT A CAMP

And all this disconnectedness had me thinking
about my thinking quite often. Was I really a scientist and I just needed to get more serious about it?
Was I really an experience guy and just needed to
strip off the last vestiges of my modern days that

still clung to me? And if I wasn't thinking what I was thinking because I had deduced these ideas in a detached sort of way, and if I wasn't thinking them because some adrenaline-enriched, existentially sweaty experience emblazoned these ideas on my soul, then why did I think like I did?

I wandered as a man without a camp. When I was with old folks, I'd slip on a monocle and a lab coat and speak in apt scientific phrases. *Well, of course . . . I am convinced . . . clearly the contradictions in this conclusion*—phrases like that. When near the postmoderns, I'd give vent to my cynicism, make fun of phrases like *ultimate truth* and pretend I was all soul and heart and gut.

But now I am coming out of the closet. I am hammering my flagpole into the ground—striking a new camp! Well, not exactly. Really, I have just decided to be honest with myself. To dispense with the palette of words from the modern camp and the assumptions of the postmodern camp and just try to be honest about how I think. My thinking about thinking has gotten me to a place of curiosity. I want to look at and describe my thinking without using the frameworks of others.

Why do something so seemingly self-indulgent? Why presume to enter into the rarified air of thinking *about* thinking about thinking? Well, I only had the gumption to step into this task because of an argument I was having with a friend.

A BLESSED ARGUMENT

This friend and I were arguing about an old-fashioned idea of mine that he disagreed with. But this seemingly silly idea isn't just another casual idea; it's a real *conviction* of mine, if you will. And we'd been doing this arguing via e-mail, which you've just gotta love and you've just gotta hate.

Anyway, I sat down to defend this idea. I started defending it using the modern language I had learned early in life. *I am convinced because of the following evidence . . . And do you see the apparent contradictions in these attacks against my idea?* Stuff like that. But when it came down to it, I realized that I didn't really believe that idea because of those reasons. So I deleted the e-mail. It just wasn't honest.

Next I tried defending the conviction with postmodern language. I waxed eloquent about my *encounters* with this idea and just how much my soul *resonated* with it . . . but that too felt shallow and fake. There was something more than experience going on in my head that made me hold to this particular idea with such conviction. So, despite the clever journeying language, I deleted that e-mail too.

And was left sitting in front of my computer. Bereft of my familiar modern language, dissatisfied with my new postmodern language. But still (and this is an important point) *really believing* this idea that my friend disagreed with. I really held that conviction dearly, but I was absolutely unable to tell my friend *why* without dipping my paintbrush in preset palettes of words that weren't really my reasons for holding to the idea in the first place.

That was the dilemma that kicked me from thinking about my thinking into the presumptuous land of thinking about thinking about thinking. How should I think about what's going on up in my head? What words and paradigms best explain and describe what is going on up there? And how should we go about evaluating which approach to thinking about our thinking is the best?

Feeling like a man without a land, I struck out for the shoreline of honesty. Not out of courage and higher ideals, but out of desperation. I had to write my friend back and tell him why I so held to my conviction. (And I had started to grow curious myself about why I did!) But I knew that the prefabricated answers wouldn't do it. Current models and language had failed me. So I walked a lonely walk of honesty. Sound dramatic enough?

It wasn't really too dramatic. But it was enlightening and (this is another important part) *very helpful*. And a little embarrassing. The e-mail I sent my friend was received graciously, but I know it was strange. And a little simplistic. And . . . *silly* maybe. Something that would likely get laughed out of both of my previous camps.

But that's my brain for you. It's not like a scientific lab, and it's not like a mountain bike ride. It's just not. It's more like a house, I found out. A house full of living ideas.

A GIFT OF WORDS

Whether you want to take a tour of my noggin out of voyeuristic curiosity (*Ooh, look at this poor guy's head*) or because your own thinking has left you thinking about thinking (*Boy, I don't really feel at home in either of these camps either*), I am offering this tour for two personal reasons: (1) slowing down enough to give a decent tour helps me think about thinking about my thinking. Which I definitely need help with. And (2) I have a hunch it might be helpful for folks out there to have a third palette of words and metaphors to choose from. Words are powerful, I believe. And I do not offer them lightly or glibly.

This tour is a gift of words, then. And while giving a tour of my brain might "out" me and get me permanently banned from both the modern camp *and* the postmodern camp, it's a risk I am willing to take. A gift of words and phrases can be that important.

In fact, WORDS ARE POWERFUL is an idea that lives in my head. He's actually got Permanent Resident status up there. WORDS ARE POWERFUL is an idea that looks and acts like a Frenchman, with his eyes always closed in rapturous thought. He speaks with a great accent and I love to hear him tell his story during house meetings in the living room up in my head.

But I am getting ahead of myself. And likely confusing you. Which means it's now time to leave the calm visitor's center and enter the realm of my head.

Chapter 2

WELCOME TO THE HOUSE OF LIVING IDEAS

The first thing you'll notice as you step into my head is how oddly all the ideas in there are acting. They don't behave like inanimate factoids. And they don't come across like random, nonlinear impressions from experience. They are more like people.

They're *not* people, of course. But they sure act a lot like people. They act a lot more like personalities than pieces of data, that's for sure. They each have a presence, a style that's all their own. And they are all living together in my head. A head, as it turns out, that is crowded with ideas.

A CROWDED HOUSE

An image might be helpful at this point. If you've ever lived in a crowded house, such as a dormitory in college or a house you shared with a bunch of buddies in order to save on rent, then you already know a lot about my head and how it works.

When I was nineteen, I moved onto Mount Rainier in beautiful western Washington. To be more specific, I moved into some barracks known as Employee Housing where most of the young employees working inside Mount Rainier National Park lived during the busy summer months on the mountain. There we were, a ragtag collection of personalities from across the United States all thrown into a huge "house" together for the summer.

We had to share space and interact and make friends and fight and reconcile and gossip and share stories and get along while we were all living in that crowded house. And we had to find a way to live together that was sustainable for the whole summer.

When a new guy or gal moved in partway through the summer, we would all stare at him and size him up, or we would talk with her and find out about her, listening to her stories, taking note of her accent. Eventually we would begin fitting the newcomer into our carefully (but invisibly) constructed social hierarchies.

That's kind of what it's like in my head.

When I hear a new idea, I am not encountering a dead piece of data that I can take (or not take) and examine in the sterile laboratory of my mind, in the end deciding whether or not to accept the data as "truth" and file it away in my systematized Filing Cabinet of Truth and Lies. It's not like that at all in my mind.

When I hear a new idea, it's like there's some new person moving into the house in my head. The house of living ideas, that is. And every idea up there has a certain attitude and certain posture. And each new idea tells a story. That part's important to understand. Every idea has a story to tell. That's why they come into the house in my head— to tell me their story.

Let me show you what I'm talking about. Remember that argument my friend and I were having? Well, that argument was about an old, increasingly unpopular idea that I hold pretty tightly to. That old idea is that the New Testament is a reliable, divinely inspired set of writings that were written to forever record the truth about Jesus. It'd be fair to say I believe in "the authority of Scripture."

But when I sat down to explain and defend my belief, I realized I didn't believe in the authority of Scripture because of a certain set of data I had tested. It wasn't just a scientific sort of conclusion I had come to. Nor did I come to believe it solely from experience. Not exactly.

When I was perfectly honest, I realized it was a more accurate description of my thinking to say that this idea about the Bible had, over time, *come to live within my head*. And I'd decided to let it stay. I didn't kick it out of my head. Why not? Well, because I liked the idea and the story it told and how it interacted with all the other ideas in my head.

You see, this particular idea, THE AUTHORITY OF SCRIPTURE, had a certain attitude and posture and had a certain story to tell (like all ideas do). Over the years this idea had simply walked into my head like . . . like an old man clutching a big black Bible. A somewhat silly-looking old man who was poorly dressed, gray-haired, stubborn . . . and who would not let go of that big black book in his hands for anything. He clutched it tightly to himself.

When I asked THE OLD MAN CLUTCHING THE BIG BLACK BIBLE (the name he usually goes by up in my head) why he was clutching that book so tightly, he told me his story. And even though that old man looks kind of silly, and even though many new (much nicer-looking) ideas mock him and ridicule him, I really like his story. I do. And I like the answers he gives to all the other ideas up there. And so I let him stay in my head.

It's like that in my head. It's a house of living ideas. And whenever I hear a new teaching or encounter some idea or other, that idea is walking into my crowded head, telling me its story.

WHEN IDEAS MEET

But when a new idea comes sauntering (running, skipping, slinking) into my brain, there's a whole house of living ideas already there. And so they interact. Sometimes they have questions for each other and a sort of dialogue ensues between ideas. Or maybe most of the old ideas in the house really like the new guy and get along with him just fine. But sometimes two ideas are like oil and water, and it becomes apparent to everyone in the house that one of those two ideas is going to have to move out of my head eventually.

That's what it was like on Mount Rainier. When someone new moved in, we all watched him closely for a while, sizing him up. Or we'd hear her story, then we'd start interacting (flirting, joking, arguing, gossiping) with her as we lived in Employee Housing. And that's what it's like in my head. It's that interaction (that mingling of ideas in the living room of the house) that is at the center of actual thinking up in my head.

One day, for example, a new idea called SHINY HAPPY GLOBALIZATION came walking into my head. (I was reading an article about globalization that was talking about all of the new, level playing fields that globalization is creating across the globe. And this article was very positive about this development—the future holds more hope for folks in developing countries because they can shop their resources anywhere they want via the Internet, and companies' supply chains and production operations can be spread across several countries, etc.)

Well, as I read the article, this new idea, SHINY HAPPY GLOBALIZATION, walked right into my head—with a strut. He struck me immediately as a positive, aggressive, hopeful idea. SHINY HAPPY GLOBALIZATION had gear everywhere (an earpiece cell phone in one ear, a Web-enabled laptop under his arm) and he was trilingual. Now I couldn't just sum up this idea about globalization in a phrase or propositional statement. No, this idea had a personality, an attitude. And, more importantly, he had a story to tell. Just like every idea.

But I wasn't encountering SHINY HAPPY GLO-BALIZATION in a vacuum—he was coming into an already lived-in house (there are other ideas already up there). And so, if I was actually going to "think" about this new idea (which is different from just hearing its story), I had to call a house meeting so all the current residents of the house would come into the living room and meet (and interact with) the new guy. That's thinking.

And that's what I did. I went for a walk after reading the article and let the residents upstairs start to interact. At points this thinking was casual, playful. Just like up on Rainier, some of the current residents will immediately take to the new guy. THE BEAUTY OF CROSSING CULTURES (an attractive, well-developed idea about what often happens to people when they cross cultures) smiled immediately at the new guy . . . was that a wink I saw? But other ideas were immediately suspicious. For instance, GARDEN-MAN (who is always talking about the unseen drawbacks to supposedly miraculous technological solutions to real, dirty human problems) frowned immediately and started asking SHINY HAPPY GLOBALIZATION some direct questions.

It's like that in my head. There are all kinds of different ideas: some are new, some are old; some love coming to every house meeting, others are more shy. Some have special status in my house (more on Permanent Resident status later) and some get kicked out before even getting to tell their whole story. Just like on Mount Rainier. There are all kinds of arguments, discussions and dialogues going on in my head when a new idea comes in.

A HOUSE WANTS ORDER

I realize that may sound chaotic. And I'm sure it would be like chaos, too, except for one thing: the household always finds equilibrium. After all, every house wants order.

If two ideas hate each other—they are diametrically opposed—all the ideas make sure this disagreement is taken care of. Maybe not right away. But the tension in the house is palpable and must be resolved. Just like when oil and water are poured into the same bowl. Just like on Rainier.

Once the Brown brothers (John and Jesse) started fighting that summer, it got so that they couldn't go on living in the same barracks (which happened to be the barracks I was staying in as well). One of them had to move out in order for there to be some peace in the place. We all knew it had to happen. The only question was which brother was going to find a new place to stay. If there's tension in a full house, it will get worked out. And it's like that in my head, too.

Let me give you a simple example. Early on in life, GIRLS ARE KIND OF ICKY was an idea that lived in my head. I won't bore you with the story of how that idea moved into my head. Let's just say it did. But then, as inevitably happens in life, another idea visited my head. This new idea, GIRLS CAN BE PRETTY DARNED INTERESTING, came when I saw Amy (who lived down Nichol Quarry Lane just a bit from us) wearing her red and white cowgirl outfit for Halloween one year.

Now, this new idea, GIRLS CAN BE PRETTY DARNED INTERESTING, didn't get along so well with that good old idea GIRLS ARE KIND OF ICKY. There was tension up in my head. Everyone saw how these two ideas looked at each other. And all the ideas up in my head knew that either these two ideas would have to talk out their tensions (which they did) or one of them would have to move out. Every house wants order after all. And the house in my head is no exception.

Another thing about full houses is that there are always definite (if sometimes invisible and unspoken) social hierarchies worked out among folks. Every house has a pecking order. Live with a lot of people, and you will be amazed at how quickly and unmistakably these invisible but detailed hierarchies are established. They don't have to be legislated or explicitly declared (though sometimes that happens), but they are always real and unmistakable.

Up on Mount Rainier there was this older gal named Kathryn who was doing her third summer on the mountain. Yes, her *third* summer in a row. And she got her own room. And none of us even questioned that. Now, this wasn't written down anywhere, of course. We just sensed her seniority and what it meant. And it's the same in my mind. Some ideas simply outrank others and are not shy about pushing their weight around (more about this "seniority" in chapter four).

My brain is like people living in a house: it's complex and relational and about stories, quite unlike a laboratory. But it's also governed by organic but very real order and systems, unlike the optimistic hey-can't-we-all-just-get-along salad bar of postmodern experience. That's what it's like in my head.

And since most of this action takes place when the ideas are talking with each other in the living room up in my head, it's time we sit down on one of those couches and take a closer look at what actually happens there.

Chapter 3

HANGING OUT IN
THE LIVING ROOM

The living room up in my head is great—it's where the real thinking goes on. It's great because it brings ideas into the light of day. Some ideas would prefer to stay hidden away, unquestioned, unchallenged (more on this later), which is not good for clear thinking at all. But the living room is where the ideas come into the light and talk. The living room is where things get hashed out, which, as you can imagine, can get kind of messy.

For example, one day after I had a difficult conversation with one of my coworkers, a little squirt of an idea walked into my head. CONFLICT IS ALWAYS HORRIBLE was his name. He was a little idea, but he had a story to tell, like every idea. (A side note: while some new ideas come from obvious places, such as a book or article, others come into my brain from less obvious places, maybe a conversation or experience.)

Anyway, that day, after having a difficult conversation, I was driving back home (about a two-hour drive) and that idea, CONFLICT IS ALWAYS HORRIBLE, walked into my head and right away started whispering his story to me. "Today was bad, you know. Conflict is always like that. It is poisonous and invades your very soul and rips peace away from your heart. Today was not a good day at all. People must do whatever they can to avoid the . . . the *stench* of conflict!"

This little idea reminded me of some of his little cousins, such as ABOVE ALL ELSE MAINTAIN CONTROL and EVERYONE'S OUT TO GET YOU. They've all got attitude. And they have furtive little eyes. They whisper their stories quickly, always glancing around as they do, like they're letting me in on a dangerous conspiracy that's afoot.

So while driving home I got to thinking. Which means I called a house meeting for all the ideas already living in my head to hang out with the new idea, CONFLICT IS ALWAYS HORRIBLE.

Right off the bat, SOME PEOPLE ARE INTROVERTED AND THAT'S OK walked into the room (this is a pretty developed idea about what I am like as a person). SOME PEOPLE ARE INTROVERTED AND THAT'S OK is on the shy side, but he stands his ground; he doesn't like any of the little gangster types. "Listen, just because conflict feels invasive and painful doesn't necessarily mean it is bad.

Some people, like Don, just feel conflict more deeply. And that's OK. You can't go hiding away every time you feel conflict."

But the living room is dynamic. It's rarely just two ideas interacting—it's a house meeting after all. As I drove and thought, BLESSED SLOPPYMAN chimed in right after SOME PEOPLE ARE INTRO-VERTED AND THAT'S OK. "Listen, little punk, you are assuming that messiness is inherently bad. It is not! Let me tell you a thing or two about how beau-tiful and human it is to be in messy relationships." And BLESSED SLOPPYMAN started telling *his* story again.

Then the BRILLIANCE OF COLLABORATION stood up from her couch in the corner of the living room, smiling and shaking her head. She had a thing or two to talk over with CONFLICT IS ALWAYS HORRIBLE too. And his story didn't really hold up that well as the two of them talked about the nature of collaboration and conversation and disagree-ment and conflict.

So in the end I kicked the little twerp CONFLICT IS ALWAYS HORRIBLE out, and was left with a re-newed clarity about what I think about the nature of conflict. His story had some good parts to it (conflict *is* hard), but the whole of his story was just off. The tone was not right, the ending of his story was all wrong. And the other ideas just had better stories. They held together more.

That's some of what it's like when ideas hang out in the living room up in my head. And time spent in the living room always seems to be worth it, like that day driving home. If I really spend time having a house meeting (thinking), it is always helpful.

Sometimes a new idea has a slap-fantastic story I have never heard, and some older ideas (whose stories were losing some credibility under questioning) get kicked out (like when I started reading science fiction after finishing my degree in English and SCIENCE FICTION ROCKS! came strolling into my head and got THE IMPLICIT INFERIORITY OF GENRE LITERATURE kicked out of my head altogether).

Sometimes a new idea gets talking with some of the other ideas and everyone's stories get nuanced better (like when GIRLS ARE KIND OF ICKY and GIRLS CAN BE PRETTY DARNED INTERESTING got to share notes). More flesh and detail get added to stories. And with the new idea moving in, the whole household of ideas is richer for the addition.

And sometimes a new idea just gets ditched. Just like that. But if I ditch it, it's because its story wasn't as good as the other stories. Or because his story was contradictory and the ideas up in my head just couldn't get along, couldn't live under the same roof (like when CONFLICT IS ALWAYS HORRIBLE got kicked out during my drive home).

It's a lot like a household up in my head. If a couple ideas are not getting along and are clashing in the living room, the tension will get worked out somehow. Every house wants order.

PAIN IN THE LIVING ROOM

Sometimes, though, thinking can be downright painful. Somewhere I read that Dr. Martin Luther King Jr. once said, "Nothing pains some people so much as having to think." When I heard this quote for the first time, I knew at once that PEOPLE AVOID THINKING was a nice idea. And I found out later in life why the idea's story was so true: thinking can be hard.

It's hard for many reasons. One of the many is that it can lead to cognitive dissonance. That's when there's Drama in the House! The clashes between roommates on TV's various reality shows (which seem purposefully set up to ensure juicy conflict) are nothing compared to the tension that can go on in the living room. You should see me sometimes after hearing a challenging sermon or reading a "thought-provoking" book (a whole busload of ideas all cramming in my house at once). My face is serious and I get this "Kierkegaard look" (as my wife calls it) where I am working it all out.

Call it cognitive dissonance, call it being confused, call it trying to process all this new information—whatever you call it, it still hurts. It hurts because the house is in an uproar. And everyone in the house feels the tension in the air and walks around on eggshells. Until I get the gumption to call a house meeting and work it all out.

Like the time a bright yellow bus (with the name Higher Criticism painted on the side in a really cool-looking font) pulled up and sophisticated Greek-speaking gentlemen came into the house and started picking all kinds of fights with THE OLD MAN CLUTCHING THE BIG BLACK BIBLE. Boy, were there some fireworks then! It got so crazy I ended up actually kicking THE OLD MAN out of the house. Yep, I kicked that old geezer right out of my head!

That caused some weird looks around the house, I tell ya. THE OLD MAN CLUTCHING THE BIG BLACK BIBLE had Seniority Status *and* was a Permanent Resident, after all. My house was in shambles at that point. All of the intricately worked-out social hierarchies were thrown into confusion and a period of jockeying began: What do I believe now? Who will be the new Permanent Resident? What idea would govern the others? Was any Senior Idea safe from getting kicked out?

It's a long story (too long for this tour, anyway—you can check out *The Old Man Living in My Head: One Guy's Musings About the Bible* if you are really curious), but eventually THE OLD MAN came back in and many of those guys from the bus got kicked out. At least for a while.

But that's what it's like in the living room up in
my head. It's interactive. It's confusing and painful
sometimes. But it's great. There may be ups and
downs, but in the long run I am getting a house of
better and better stories, if I but take the time to do
some thinking.

THE DIFFERENCE BETWEEN
HEARING AND THINKING

The living room is great because when I call a
house meeting, all the ideas (well, most of them)
come out and meet the new guy, listen to his story
and dialogue with him. That's when I'm thinking.

It's messy and exhilarating and loud and chaotic
and relational and complex and beautiful when all
the ideas living upstairs interact with a new idea.
But I have to be honest: that's not always happening—I'm not always thinking. Not carefully anyway.

Sometimes this is because the new idea is a
Pointy Idea and I'm just not in the mood for a
change (more on Pointy Ideas in the next chapter).
Sometimes I'm just lazy or distracted or too busy.

But even when I'm not taking the time to think,
new ideas are still walking into the house of living
ideas—it happens whenever I read a book, watch a
show, talk with someone, get barraged with seduc-
tive advertisements, and so on. But if I'm not
taking the time to *think* about these new ideas
(hearing their full story, inviting other ideas to

cross-examine them), then they just hang around in my head. Which means they are there and they affect the house in some way . . . but I'm not paying attention to them. (A dangerous state of affairs, I've found out.)

This is one of the things that has been so helpful about thinking about how I think: I've begun to realize the difference between hearing something and really thinking about it. I've begun to realize my need to call the ideas out for a house meeting and take time to just think.

But as great as the living room is, things get weird if I'm not remembering that not all ideas are created equal. There are all sorts of ideas up there, and some of them affect me and my head differently than others. And since those differences are important to note, that'll be the next stop on our tour.

A MENU OF
COMMON FLAVORS

I keep mentioning different types of ideas. I might as well give you a tour through the types of ideas that make it into my house, describing some general characteristics of each. This brief cataloging of ideas should clarify quite a bit about how thinking happens up in my head.

Like any house, it's unfair and simplistic to completely generalize all the occupants. But even though every idea is different and unique, there truly are some different categories, or flavors, of ideas. And this would be a shoddy tour if I didn't at least give you a brief overview of some of the major types I've got roaming around upstairs.

SENIOR IDEAS
Some ideas have been upstairs in my head for quite some time. For example, THE PRECIOUS GOLD OF BOOKS has been in my head since I was old enough

to encounter books and to think about what that encounter was like. THE PRECIOUS GOLD OF BOOKS tells a story about how wonderful it is to read, how surprising it is to read, what good companions books can become. This was one of the first ideas to move into my head when I was a child and it still lives up there.

And the truth is, the longer an idea is around, the more seniority it has. It gets the bigger bedroom; it gets more respect in the living room. Any new ideas visiting my head can tell which ideas practically own the house, and they tend to tread lightly when near these Senior Ideas. Like a sophomore in college moving into a shared house—no one has to tell that sophomore that the fifth-year senior gets special privileges; he just knows it.

Something else you should know about Senior Ideas, though, is that I've heard their stories so many times that they just start to sound "right." Like a poet who reads his poetry to himself too many times, the words and phrases become so familiar that they sound *inevitable,* almost perfect.

Now, this can happen to a poet regardless of whether he's written a good poem or not. Hear it enough and it starts sounding inherently right, and editing or changing it seems unfathomable. It's the same with these ideas. Senior Ideas may be hogwash, but they sound right. This is something I have to keep an eye out for. Senior Ideas have been kicked out of the house before, but I tell ya, the process was painful.

POINTY IDEAS

Some ideas tell a story that makes me cringe. Not because it's a bad story, necessarily, but because it is going to cost me something. And I can just sense it. These ideas tell stories that disrupt the mood of the house.

Maybe all the ideas and I are getting pretty comfortable; hierarchies have been worked out and I (and my comfortable head) am getting nicely drowsy in the house on a warm Saturday afternoon. But then some little idea comes knocking (maybe I was reading a book or talking with someone new or watching a movie I had never seen before) and I just have a sense that this new idea is gonna tell a story that gets all my comfortable ideas in a hissy fit. This is significant because I am naturally predisposed against these ideas.

For example, I remember the first time Mc-DONALD'S JUST MIGHT BE EVIL came strolling into my head. I was learning about rainforests and what's done to rainforests so that McDonald's can have places to raise cheap cattle. But I really, really like McDonald's French fries. (Really.) So I sent Mc-DONALD'S JUST MIGHT BE EVIL packing and kept enjoying my French fries as usual.

But then I was listening to people talk about a

new book on fast food in America. And there he was—that pesky idea had gotten into my head again. Well, I turned him out for the second time. I just don't like ideas that are pointy.

But then I heard about a documentary about a man who ate only at McDonald's for a month . . . and almost died. And there he was: McDONALD'S JUST MIGHT BE EVIL was sitting in my head again!

But McDONALD'S JUST MIGHT BE EVIL is a Pointy Idea. And so I tend to be biased against it. With some Pointy Ideas, I don't even want to let them in my head at all. Maybe I kick them out without ever calling a house meeting in the living room. Maybe I have a house meeting, but it's a kangaroo court—we're all predisposed against the new idea's story and we all take a quick vote and kick the sucker out without really doing any thinking. (And my love of French fries gets to stay.) Pointy Ideas have ended up staying in the house at times, but it's always . . . well, *pointy*.

SUGAR IDEAS

Some ideas that come into my head are the exact opposite of Pointy Ideas: they stroke me; they gratify me in some way; they make my life easier. They bring a message of peace. These ideas are usually pretty conspicuous: their stories are almost always lame. They rarely tell a story that is believable or real sounding or that holds any sort of substance.

But they tickle my pleasure. They promise ease somehow. And these ideas, as you might expect, tend to persuade me much more easily than they should. If I am predisposed against Pointy Ideas (even though they may have the best story around), I am also predisposed *toward* Sugar Ideas (even though their story may be grossly wrong and silly).

For example, A HOT ORDER OF McDONALD'S FRIES ALWAYS MAKES YOU HAPPY is a Sugar Idea. There's no real substance to the story (although THAT WHICH IS FAMILIAR IS ALWAYS PREFERABLE will always cheer at the telling of that French fry story), and many ideas living in my head can rip the story to shreds. But I am predisposed toward that idea because . . . well, because it's a Sugar Idea!

I have to remember how Sugar Ideas affect my thinking or else I tend to have all sorts of them move into my head, and the place (in the long run) turns into an absolute mess. This is especially important because Sugar Ideas are so prevalent these days. And because I become enamored with them so quickly.

PERMANENT RESIDENTS

There are some ideas that I give special status to. In particular, for various reasons, there are some ideas that I not only let stay in my house (I like their story) but also that I hold as *deep convictions*. They are so meaningful, their stories so "right," that I make a sort of covenant with them. I will never kick you out, I say. This is usually a conscious decision on my part, but sometimes slowly over time an idea becomes so powerful in my mind, becomes so dominant over other ideas, that it takes on Permanent Resident status implicitly.

For example, THE AUTHORITY OF SCRIPTURE, that old man I've already mentioned, has Permanent Resident status. I so like his story (and his responses to the questions other ideas pepper him with) that I have granted him this special status. And his having that status affects the whole house of living ideas.

Permanent Residents are important because they hold great sway in the living room. If some new idea is telling a story that contradicts one of my Permanent Residents, I am usually going to side with the Permanent Resident. Usually. And the debate usually won't even last long.

Having Permanent Residents brings a great amount of order to the house. These privileged ideas have authority that allows them to kick new ideas out quickly, and being the highest in the hierarchy of the house, they bring order to my head. The house in my head is a tiny bit like a democracy (all ideas can at least start telling their story), but in a lot of ways it's much more ordered than that (some ideas have permission to throw their weight around).

This doesn't mean a Permanent Resident can't have her story challenged (it frequently is) or be demoted (this does happen from time to time) or even be kicked out (something that's a real, painful possibility, like the time I kicked THE OLD MAN out). But it does mean they are a special class of ideas. And that means something for the house of ideas in my head. (If you are wondering how I decide who gets to be a Permanent Resident, then you're asking a wonderful question we'll get to in the next chapter.)

BACK DOOR IDEAS

This may or may not surprise you, but in my head there are some ideas that did not come in the front door. Yeah, doesn't seem right. But so it is. Some ideas find their way into my head through a back door left ajar or through an open window, or maybe they came into my head when the house was still being constructed.

Almost all ideas that are members of the gang known as Received Certainties from My Culture are fine examples of Back Door Ideas. These are ideas that are so prevalent, so common, so present in the air I breathe that I start assuming these ideas, without ever really thinking about them or asking them questions or seeing if their stories really amount to much. Some of the members of this gang include PAIN IS BAD, EASE IS GOOD, WAITING IS UNFAIR,

MEMBERS OF YOUR FAMILY ARE MORE IMPOR-
TANT THAN ANYONE ELSE, EDUCATION IS VALU-
ABLE and RETIREMENT IS A NECESSITY.

These assumed ideas may have good stories or
bad stories, but their assumed status (the fact that
they are Back Door Ideas) makes them a bit dangerous. They are dangerous because they are definitely
in my head (they affect all of my thinking, since
they are living somewhere in the house), and yet
they so rarely come to the living room, so rarely
have to defend their own stories.

They tend to be somewhat vaporous, hiding in
back rooms and basement closets. The problem
with that is that I don't get to think about them and
really decide whether they get to stay or have to
leave. These ideas are dangerous, then.

Because of Back Door Ideas, I have to remind
myself to not just call a house meeting and assume that all the ideas in my head are present,
but I have to beat some pots and pans in the hidden corners of my head to get these received, insidious ideas to come out and show themselves.
Ideas such as LIGHTER SKIN IMPLIES GREATER IN-
TELLIGENCE, PORNOGRAPHY IS REALLY HARM-
LESS IN THE END and WHAT HAPPENS ON OTHER
CONTINENTS DOESN'T REALLY MATTER prefer to
remain hidden. Thinking about things that are
normally just assumed is tough business. But really important.

SEXY IDEAS

Some ideas come in with a swagger that is intoxicating. Just like SHINY HAPPY GLOBALIZATION, these ideas sound cool, look cool and are often coming from somewhere really cool. Before ever really hearing their story or asking them questions or allowing other ideas to interact with them, I start liking them. These are ideas like THE WEB IS THE ANSWER and DA VINCI HAD A NAUGHTY LITTLE SECRET. These sexy ideas are usually dressed very hip. They often come into my head from the latest book, the latest magazine, the latest genius-of-the-hour.

I know I should guard myself against these ideas, try not to fall in love with them immediately without really thinking about them. But that's tough. Their form and style and new-car smell is intoxicating and they can make even Permanent Residents look like old fuddy-duddies who are silly. Even if the real silliness is in their own story. Knowing about this class of ideas can help shake off the intoxication of their new-car smell just long enough to remember that I'm not supposed to just smile and nod at new ideas but actually think about them.

MANY TYPES OF IDEAS

Lots of different types of ideas live in my head and walk through my head and throw a sleeping bag down in some room in my head hoping to stay a while. Not only do ideas have very different stories to tell (some good, some terrible, some silly), but they also posture themselves in very different ways, naturally affecting me in very different ways.

To think, along with my modern friends, that all ideas are lined-up inert pieces of data is to ignore this posturing of ideas and the ways they affect me. To think, along with my postmodern friends, that all ideas—if sincerely held and experienced—are valid is to ignore how bad some ideas can be even if I am predisposed to "resonate" with them. It also ignores the real hierarchies that exist among ideas.

The ideas in my head are like people living in a house. And it's important to know that there are lots of different flavors of them.

But this brings us to the point in the tour for a little Q&A. Some of you have been patiently holding your hands up, so I figure it's time to call on a few of you.

Chapter 5

FREQUENTLY
ASKED QUESTIONS

....

As you wander around inside my head and hear me talking about how it all goes up there, there are likely some questions popping into your head. Allow me to answer some of the most frequently asked questions I get about my house of living ideas.

Does it really feel like that in your head?
The reality is, this is a tour of my thinking. And thinking is something that works at an entirely different speed than we're used to contemplating. My head (and all these ideas, debates, conversations, storytellings, cross-examination periods and so on) is working at a speed our physical bodies can barely comprehend—it's a blur of activity. (OK, in my head maybe it's a little less of a blur than with most people, but it is a blur nonetheless.)

It's kind of like rain falling on a grassy field. Videotape it and play it back in super duper slow-mo and you see that all of the apparent random splattering and chaos of the rain really is something quite intricate and complex and beautiful, governed by the laws of physics. It's kind of like that on this tour—we're slowing everything way down.

So, no. My thinking doesn't feel *exactly* like what I am describing here. But the more I've begun to reflect on my thinking (slowing it down a bit), the more I can honestly say that what I have been describing for the last few chapters really is a close approximation of how I think. It really happens like that.

What about emotions and your heart?

This right here, of course, is not a tour of my heart. Or of my soul, my body or anything else for that matter. Just my upstairs. And if you think that as I've gone along I'm blurring the lines between the brain and these other parts, then you've got a good sniffer. Because I am.

Why do I like one story over another? The answer to that question would take us through every part of me—even parts of me I don't know so much about myself. It's not just my brain that likes an idea; it's my heart, my soul, my body even. My brain has a special job of being the house and helping to sort out the stories and hear all the questions and objections, but it's ultimately *all of me* that likes a story. Or doesn't. It's all of me that sides with one idea over another.

It's my brain that makes sure I'm hearing the story right, that forces the idea who's telling that story to sit down on the couch and take some questions from the other ideas. The brain is the house and arena for all of that.

Sometimes I hear people talking about how their "mind" believes something but their "heart" is slow to believe it. I've even said that myself from time to time. But now that I've gotten to thinking about thinking more, I figure what's really going on is that an idea has gotten into the house (you could say I believe it), but I just don't like its story (really, I *don't* believe it).

Confusing enough? Here's a real-life example. I remember the first time I honestly admitted that even though I *believed* that God loved me, I had a hard time *feeling* that with my heart. At the time it seemed like a difference between what I believed and what I felt. A battle between my head and my heart. But now I'd say it's more that GOD LOVES ME had moved into my head, but YOU ARE NOT LOVABLE was another idea already living up there!

And while it was true, in one sense, that I "believed" God loved me (that idea was in my head), it was also true that I "believed" that I was not lovable (that idea was also living up there). And for whatever reason, YOU ARE NOT LOVABLE's story kept winning out. I think my wounded heart made me predisposed against GOD LOVES ME. And so YOU ARE NOT LOVABLE had Seniority Status and GOD LOVES ME kept being put in its place in the living room in my head. Or it kept getting kicked out of my head. Or something like that.

If that sounds confusing, you're getting the picture. My heart is often very involved in pushing me toward or away from an idea in ways I don't always know about or understand.

Is your faith involved in the same way?

Yes and no. Yes, because my faith is very involved in how I end up liking or not liking an idea. And my faith (it'd be fair to look at my faith and call me an "evangelical Christian") gives me a new source of ideas, a source that I trust more than other sources. In my case, this is the Bible.

THE OLD MAN CLUTCHING THE BIG BLACK BIBLE is an idea that came into my head as I was becoming a Christian. And this singular idea—that God has chosen to create a book that is authoritative and carries his voice to us—has affected my thinking more deeply and more comprehensively than anything else.[1]

It affects me because I have a book that I trust. And as I carefully read this book, I am encountering a stream of ideas that I have prejudged as being fit to live in my head. (Even though these ideas

must still tell their stories, still interact with the
current residents of my head, still answer questions in the living room . . . and even get kicked
back out.) And this source of trustworthy ideas is a
book I return to again and again, trying to fill my
own house of living ideas with the ideas found in its
pages.

This, of course, is one aspect of faith that turns
many secularists away from religion. They can't
imagine submitting themselves in such a way to
one source. And they, perhaps wrongly, assume
that this means giving up the task of thinking altogether. But for many people of faith, whether
Christian or not, our thinking is deeply affected by
having such a source of trustworthy, "true" ideas.

*I thought you said "Yes and no"–does your faith affect
your thinking in ways your heart does not?*
Oh right. Well, being a Christian affects my thinking by providing me with a source of trustworthy
ideas and by giving me clear direction in working
out the hierarchies among ideas in my head. But
there is one other way in which my faith affects my
thinking. (This is an experience I am not as confi-
dent is shared by people of other faiths.)

You see, in becoming a Christian, I invited the
Spirit of God to blow into me and swirl around inside me. This divine spiritual presence affects every
part of me. Including my thinking. As one of the

earliest Christians described it, once this Spirit re-
sides within us, we are no longer conformed to the
ways of the world, but our minds are renewed.[2]

So not only does my faith give me a trusted
source for ideas and give me clear direction for
which ideas are more important and lasting and
true, but it also brings the Spirit of God into con-
tact with this house of living ideas.

Maybe it's as if a strong, beautiful wind has
started to blow throughout this house of my mind
and to change the feel of the place (and the smell of
the place) over time. My guess is that this wind
pushes away certain ideas and makes my head more
welcoming to other ideas, having a cleansing effect
over time.

So, do you believe there is such a thing as Truth?

Yes, I think there is. And it is something my head
hungers for.

You see, I think the reason I've been given this
brain is to get the ideas hanging out together and
interacting, not just sitting politely near each
other, silently respecting each other's space. I
know my head would never stand for that. The
ideas *are going to* interact and disagree and cross-
examine each other up in my head. And that's
what's so exhilarating about thinking. That's why I
actually believe in thinking. Because even though
my head wants peace (to have every idea who's in

the house getting along fine), *even more so* it wants
good stories. Better stories. A stronger, more fasci-
nating, interesting, resonating, intellectually stim-
ulating, well-told, honest story.

I think that Truth (yes, capital T) is the best story
out there. Not because the story is clever or witty
but because it is *the* story (singular) that tells it all.
The metastory, if you will. The Story that is the
most believable story ever, that can take in every little story and have it make sense in the scope of everything. Truth (with a capital T) is really The Story
(with a capital T and S).

So searching for truth or being on a quest for
truth is (in my head) like looking for the one Grand
Story that tells it all. The Story that is meaningfully
contradicted by no little ideas, that satisfies my
mind, that resonates with reality, that tells about
me and you and all of the little stories around.

Do you really think such a story exists?
That's a pretty big question. The fact that my head
hungers for it makes me think it does exist, just as
my thirst points to the existence of water.

And let me also throw in here that THE OLD MAN
CLUTCHING THE BIG BLACK BIBLE (who has been
reinstated as a Permanent Resident up in my head)
reads to me from his old book about one who came
as (get this) *The Story*. An actual human being who
was The Grand Story. That old man reads some

wild stuff from that book of his. And I believe that wild one.

Does this all mean that you think some people are "wrong" in what they believe or think?

Sure. Though I probably wouldn't put *wrong* in quotation marks. Some ideas tell stories that are just that. Wrong. Now, before you start thinking I'm a mean guy, let's face it—there are some ideas that tell terrible stories. And if that adjective is a bit too harsh for you, you obviously haven't met some of the limping, twisted ideas I've had stay up in my house (some for way too long!).

Granted, every idea in the midst of telling its story sounds passionate and reasoned and . . . *right*. But that's what ideas are supposed to do. That's their job. And they tell the same story so many times that they get pretty good at telling their story—whether it's a good story or not. Every idea unto itself has a sort of internal logic. Every idea. But it's when the ideas start interacting with each other that we begin to see their deficiencies.

For example, almost every time I watch TV or a movie I'll eventually have IT'S ALL IN THE KISS stroll into my head. IT'S ALL IN THE KISS is a romantic idea: she's dressed nicely and can tilt her head in a way that makes everything she does or says sound a little more credible and pure and . . . right.

But her story is terrible. You've heard it, I'm sure: there's a magical, invisible pairing of men and women on this planet and the only way to peer into the magic and find out who your special partner is . . . that's right! The Kiss. The Kiss that tells you, magically—in a moment of passion and shared saliva and smeared glasses—if the person on the other side of your tongue really is that special someone you are destined to be with forever.

It really is a silly story she tells when you stop to think about it. And very few of the ideas living in my head get along with her. It's a lopsided affair when she gets questioned about her story in the living room in my head.

The truth is, some ideas just have terrible stories to tell. And eventually (whether quickly or slowly or repeatedly) they will leave my head behind. My head is like a house—and it wants order. And her presence in there rubs against so many ideas already living there in such a bad way that she eventually leaves. Or the rest kick her out. Or something like that.

But that's a bit unfair. What about more serious ideas? Do you also believe other people's deepest convictions can be wrong?
Absolutely. The reality is, some ideas, even popular or religious or spiritual ideas, have terrible stories to tell.

Some ideas that seem to hold a lot of sway in other people's heads (real convictions) always end up getting kicked out of my head for one reason or another. These ideas may get a lot of airtime these days, and they may even be given Permanent Resident status in many people's heads, but I just can't seem to get those ideas to stay long in my head. They keep getting kicked out. Or leaving on their own.

Isn't that just plain arrogance on your part?

I guess it could be. But I can't help having ideas interact when I'm thinking, and some of them end up feeling really uncomfortable in my house of living ideas. Some of them sound silly as they tell their story.

For example, ALL RELIGIONS ARE THE SAME. You've met that idea, I'm sure. You can recognize him from a mile away. He's the guy wearing a yarmulke on his head, a cross necklace around his neck, a yin-yang tattoo on each shoulder, a Tibetan Buddhist robe over his body and a Sikh sword strapped to his waist. He looks ridiculous to me.

And I think it's his bag o' books—that drawstring bag that he carries absently in one hand—that most frustrates many of the ideas who live in my head. A drawstring bag just doesn't seem the right way to carry books around. And come to think of it, I have never actually seen him open that sack and read any of the books it contains. He says he has a copy of the Koran in there. And the Bible and the Torah and the Mishnah and the Tao Te Ching and the Book of Mormon and a couple Scientology novels.

He waves that bag around a lot (which seems not the greatest way to treat books to me) while he's telling his story. I'm sure you've heard his story before. It's about how all religions are really, when it comes down to it (a phrase he uses a lot), saying the same things. All religions are one. And if we would but focus on the basics of each religion, we would see that they are all really teaching the same thing. Namely, something about love and Valentine's Day. Or just love. Or something like that.

His story is horrendous. All of the religious ideas living in my head (from studies in Christianity, Islam, Taoism, Judaism and Wicca and friendships with many religious people) just stare at ALL RELIGIONS ARE THE SAME and his yarmulke and cross necklace and yin-yang tattoos. He really does look ridiculous. And from the way many ideas stare at him in my head, I get the impression that they are not impressed with his story and that they take offense at how he is treating their sacred texts in that drawstring bag of his.

Most of the time he leaves without anyone's saying a word. The disgusted stares are enough. At other times he will get quite a flurry of questions (none of which he has very convincing answers for, it seems to me) before making a beeline for the front door of my head. And he is gone.

There are some terrible stories out there. Terrible ones. I know myself and my own house of living ideas too well to entertain the idea (for long, anyway) that all stories are created equal.[3]

That's why I kick some ideas right out of my head. To pretend to be a housekeeper any other way seems strange to me.

But now I'm getting into some deep waters. Waters filled with weighty, wonderful questions. Questions like: How should I keep this house in my head? And what is the ultimate point of my upstairs? And which ideas do I let in? And kick out? And give Permanent Resident status to?

Good questions. Fabulous new questions that I get to ask now that I am being more honest with myself about how I think. Deep questions about this great privilege and dilemma of having been given a head.

Chapter 6

ON HAVING BEEN
GIVEN A HEAD

Being honest about how my head works has been very helpful for me.

When I think about my thinking using the pre-set modern or postmodern palettes of words, I am left trying to think like someone else. Which I am not very good at, it turns out. But when I allow myself to be perfectly honest about my thinking, it allows me to ask some good questions about how to go about thinking well.

For example, I've already told you about the different types of ideas that make their way into my head. Admitting this allows me to ask some fabulous questions: What kind of idea am I dealing with here? Does this idea have a really great story, or am I just being suckered in? Is there some idea in my head that just snuck in and I've never really thought about it explicitly? These are fabulous questions. They allow me to think fruitfully.

There are other questions that this new (though somewhat awkward) palette of words allows me to ask as well.

What kind of housekeeper should I be?

In real life sometimes I am a tidy housekeeper (just ask my kids) and sometimes I can be sloppy (just ask my wife). And it's the same in my head. At times I am tending to the house of living ideas with great care—I can be very thoughtful. I go on long walks, play hoops in some lonely park all by myself, scratch away in a journal. These are ways I tend to the house, getting the ideas to come into the living room and talk, interact, argue, whatever.

Usually I do more thinking (calling house meetings) when I've encountered a new idea that is starting to cause stress in the house. Or when there are lots of new ideas coming in together. I get a palpable sense that I need some time to process, which for me really means calling a house meeting and listening to the living ideas interact.

But sometimes I am not such a great housekeeper. Maybe I am not encountering any new ideas. Maybe all of my thoughts are drowsy and have slunk off to their bedrooms for some sleep. Maybe I have a sneaking suspicion that the new idea that crawled in last week and went quickly down to the basement is going to cause some real problems if I get around to thinking about it. So I delay a meeting, just let the ideas duke it out in my subconscious (they have been known to call meetings during my sleep), or maybe I distract myself with something else.

I think I am always thinking, but sometimes it is quite passive and slow moving. It's only when I call a house meeting and get the ideas to work it out that I make much progress.

But quick and fruitful thinking isn't always guaranteed. Sometimes I need to let the ideas live together for a while to get to know each other better. To see what the new idea is really all about. Eventually we'll get around to it, but time often helps. It gives us more data, more time to make up our minds about the new guy. At times during a heated debate I have to call a recess and admit I'm just not going to get it all thunk out just then.

What's my goal as a person with a head?

This is another good question I get to contemplate when thinking about my thinking. I rarely used to think about the goal of my thinking. But now that I am reflecting more on my upstairs, it begs this important question: As I go about my thinking, what am I trying to achieve? Or rather, what *should* I be trying to achieve?

Is having a peaceful house my goal? If so, I will want to be careful about what ideas I encounter—I wouldn't want just any old idea opening the front door and walking around in my head. It could mess things up, cause some ruckus. If my goal is lack of conflict, lack of painful debates, then that has implications for what I do with my house and how often I let new ideas in (What magazines do I read? What books do I read? Do I really want to talk with that strange person at the coffee shop about his beliefs?).

Is maintaining blessed stasis (the exact current list of residents) my goal as a thinker? If so, I will definitely want to guard my front door. Hang up a No Solicitors sign and leave the porch light off. If my goal is to forever maintain (at all costs) the current ideas I have living upstairs, then I will want to limit the amount of strange new ideas that come tramping in my house with their dirty shoes and odd stories.

Is my goal to live an easy life? If so, I should try to encounter as many Sugar Ideas as possible (mostly read advertisements and fluffy stuff) and avoid Pointy Ideas at all costs (no, I don't think I'd like to take a trip to a Third World country—thanks anyway). If this is my goal, I will want to assemble a house full of self-serving ideas. Luckily, these are plentiful (especially here in the United States). And luckily, I am already so predisposed toward Sugar Ideas that this goal is something I have a good shot at achieving.

Is my goal to find Truth? If my goal is to have a

house full of the *best* stories around, this means a few things for me. It means, first, that I will continually be allowing new ideas in so that the overall makeup of the house can always be improving.

It also means that I'll want to submit every idea to a rigorous living room dialogue: I will want to test every idea so that only the ones with the better stories can stay. That way the house is shifting and jockeying, always keeping the better story so that over time the house is full of better and better stories.

It further means that I will want to think often and well. You see, the more thinking I do, the more all of me gets to interact with the ideas: my heart and soul and body. This kind of thinking should ultimately be leading to better ideas that tell more ultimately satisfying ideas.

And finally, if this really is my goal, it means I will need to be super vigilant about Sugar Ideas, Permanent Residents, Sexy Ideas—anything that could be swaying me to allow lesser ideas to stay in my head.

Why do I even need to have a goal as a thinker? Well, the reality is that I'll be encountering new ideas all the time. I just will. Being thoughtful about what it means to think well is pretty important then. Knowing why I have been given a house of living ideas helps me live well because it guides how I deal with the constant stream of new ideas I will inevitably encounter in life.

Who do I grant Permanent Resident status to?

This is a super question for me. When I admit that there are some ideas that will get to strut around more and boss other ideas around more and be questioned less, it allows me to ask the very important question of what ideas, exactly, I give that kind of authority to.

What mere ideas get to become actual *convictions* or *beliefs* or even *adamantly held beliefs?* I don't want to confer this status too easily or quickly. It's a little like tattoos—you don't want to pull the trigger too quick on getting a tattoo. (You may really be into that guy, but you might want to hold off on tattooing his name on your butt for just a little bit.) Similarly, I should confer Permanent Resident status sparingly. Having convictions does bring great order to the house in my head, but I want to make sure it's the kind of order I want

For me this is something that takes place over time. For example, when THE OLD MAN CLUTCHING THE BIG BLACK BIBLE first walked into my head, he came highly recommended from folks I trusted. And early on, that was enough for me. I let him stay even though he did seem a bit old-fashioned to be in my head. But the more I read the Bible and began living as if its stories and sentences were true, the more I began to find unexpected things, such as healing and purpose, in my life. So, over time, my heart and body got involved and THE

OLD MAN started getting more seniority up there.

And over time, the more I see that old guy in debates with other ideas in the living room, the more I see him attacked, the more I hear his answers and his story . . . the more I like him. His answers make sense. His story seems consistent. And I see really good stuff in my life that comes from his having sway up in my head. I like that big black book he clutches. It seems to be real and honest and true.[1] And it's that kind of stuff that, over time, earns Permanent Resident status for an idea in my head. It involves all of me and usually takes time.

Switching out deeply held convictions is messy business, so I don't go about granting that privileged status on a regular basis. But I also don't float through life pretending that I hold everything loosely. There *are* going to be Permanent Residents in my head, so I might as well be explicit and purposeful about what those are. On top of all this, I continually remind myself that even deeply held convictions can be questioned—and should be questioned.

How do I get ideas into the living room for a house meeting?
This is another way of saying, how do I think? It's tempting at times to mistake hearing ideas with thinking about ideas. But thinking is the actual interaction of ideas with each other. Knowing that leads me to this very important question: how do I

get ideas into the living room?

In part this means figuring out how my house works and what allows the ideas to get together. For me it means taking time, going on a walk, washing dishes, driving in my car. If I sit still, I can't think very well. I get sort of constipated in my mind. For me it takes some kind of steady, fairly boring physical rhythm to coax all these ideas upstairs to come out and start interacting. I have many friends, though, who say that talking with someone else is what helps them. Their heads and jaws are connected somehow.

But I also like to be vigilant about the back door and open windows and all that. We are all so tempted to have blind spots, to be so "home blind" to something, that we don't really see all of these insidious assumptions that have moved into our brains. Getting ideas to the living room (all ideas) means doing careful self-analysis, having purposeful self-reflection. Actually thinking about assumptions is tough business.

Which is why other people are so helpful to me. If I am talking with others about ideas, they will often be in a better position to notice my blind spots, to notice explicitly what I only assume, especially if who I am talking to is different than me. (I can see THE BEAUTY OF CROSSING CULTURES smiling now!) Talking with others is a fabulous way to get all my ideas into the living room and is, at times, much more fruitful than sitting by myself some-where, trying to get it all worked out.

How do I talk with others about their ideas?

I'm really glad I've begun thinking about thinking more explicitly, because the more I reflect on this one question (How do I talk with others about ideas?), the more my conversations with others are becoming natural and relaxed and fruitful.

You see, there are a couple ways I've seen people talk about ideas that just have never been fun for me. And this new language for understanding and talking about ideas has helped me understand more clearly why I've never liked those two ways of talking with others about ideas. There's Waging Gang War and Visiting a Museum, and both are dis-satisfying ways of talking about ideas, if you ask me.

To Wage Gang War, you simply round up your "gang" of ideas (all the ideas living in your head) and attack someone else's gang of ideas. It's all-out war. It's debate. And it's ugly. When I am Waging Gang War, my goal is to show how silly and weak your ideas are, how your ideas wilt in the presence of my amazing gang of ideas. My goal is victory. And so is yours. And so we use our ideas as weap-ons, to attack. My goal is to shove my ideas into your head. My war cry is "You will like these ideas of mine!" And I scream this war cry as I shove my ideas into your head and use them to slay any unfortunate ideas that may have set up residence in there.

I'm not making a point about the beauty of dialogue or conversation or engaging ideas (as I think you'll soon see). I am talking about war. I am talking about a posture of talking with others about ideas that is aggressive and devoid of respect and human kindness and many other good things. I am talking about a common way of talking about ideas that I think is dirty and ugly. Waging Gang War is not something I recommend. But this doesn't mean I recommend Visiting a Museum either.

Visiting a Museum is a posture of dialogue in which each of our ideas remain distant, untouchable. When it comes to ideas, I'll show mine if you show yours. But hands off! Our ideas are for display only, inert specimens that we can display and view in respect. Just stand at a distance and smile and nod. But don't you dare step past the velvet rope barrier and actually play with any of these ideas! Often we settle for Visiting a Museum after a season that was too full of Waging Gang Wars. It seems a more peaceful, respectful way of talking about ideas.

My problem is that I find both of these ways of talking with my neighbors to be thin. And unsatisfying. And pointless. And, to be frank, my mind is bored with both of those postures. But the thing is, I think there's another way. A third way to talk with each other about ideas. A way that is much more satisfying and substantive and honest. I think of it, not as Waging Gang War or Visiting a Museum, but rather as Introducing Our Families.

An image is called for here.

Have you ever had two circles of people come together for a day? This often happens at Thanksgiving. If you've ever invited some of your family to spend Thanksgiving with another family (say, your spouse's family), then you know the dynamic I'm talking about.

You get both families together in one room, make introductions and let everybody hang out. They talk, ask each other questions, start to tell their stories to each other. By the time the pumpkin pies come out, there's usually been plenty of laughter and stories and arguments and awkward moments and hushed moments of respectful silence as the old-timers tell their stories again in feeble voices.

When we sit down to coffee and talk about ideas, that's a little more like what I think we should be doing. I may know my own family more, and I probably like my family more, but I want our two families of ideas to really interact. I want a way to talk that involves respect *and* honesty. I want real interaction. I don't mind messes; I don't mind if some of our ideas don't get along so well. But I want that to happen out in the open, around a table of hospitality.

Don't shove ideas at me, OK? And don't just flash ideas at me and not let me touch them. Let's really interact. Let's sit down together and let the laughter and stories and hushed silences and arguments happen. And then let's have some pumpkin pie.

I don't know if that makes much sense or not. But living this way among my friends and neighbors has given me great freedom to talk about ideas in a fresh, new way. It's a way of talking that involves tension. And even conflict. But it's been way more fruitful. And it allows me to be honest about what I believe and to disagree with others and have others disagree with me—all in a way that allows us to actually engage with ideas, not just aggressively attack with them or passively flash them.

And I find that engaging with ideas is the whole point.

There are plenty of other questions that being more honest about how I think allows me to ask. Questions like: How often do I question Senior Ideas? What Sugar Ideas are living up there these days? What Pointy Ideas have I been unfairly kicking out without even listening to their stories? I'm sure there are plenty of other fabulous questions rolling around in your head by now as well.

It's these great new questions that make me so glad I decided to start thinking about how I think about my head. While entering into this task has seemed silly and overly self-indulgent and conspicuously artistic at times, it has turned out to be practical and helpful in a simple, everyday way.

I'm glad I got into that e-mail argument with my friend about the authority of Scripture. His questions and honesty have led to great quantities of honesty and fruitful questions in my own life. And I'm hoping that a little of this might spill over into your life as well. Honesty and fruitful questions are worthwhile, rare commodities to possess these days. May you, the reader, be rich in them.

CONCLUSION:
YOUR HEAD

But enough about my head. The tour is officially over. My hope really is that this new palette of words is helpful to you as you deal with your own head.

Perhaps this new metaphor for thinking will allow you to reflect on your own upstairs in more helpful ways. Understanding how we think is a great gift. And a great place to start. Perhaps you, too, will be able to ask some fabulous new questions about your own thinking process.

And with clarity about our heads often comes a more fruitful way to talk with others about the ideas living up in their heads. I certainly hope this is the case for you. I hope you end up in all sorts of interesting conversations you never would have had—with your friends and neighbors and family members and that blogger you disagree with . . .

I know that this new way of thinking about thinking has, for me, led to all sorts of fruitful and exhilarating and funny conversations I never would have had otherwise.

And in these conversations I've been able to more honestly describe what I believe and what I don't believe. Why do I believe in the Bible? Do I really believe in judgment and hell? Why can't I just believe that everyone can be right no matter what they believe? I've had a much clearer and more relaxed time talking about my own beliefs and thoughts, and this has been tremendously invigorating.[1]

But as I said, enough about my head.

I hope this odd little book has indeed been of service to you, the reader. My hope is that you develop a love of ideas, a love of reflection, a love of dialoguing with others about ideas and an irrepressible love for deeply satisfying stories.

Be a thinker. For without explicitly tending to our houses of living ideas, they inevitably become a mess. Just like our physical houses. Ignore the house, and you get messiness and clutter and odd smells emanating from some unknown source. Tend to your house, and everything seems to go better—fewer messes, more calm, more peace of mind. Literally.

Happy thinking . . .

NOTES

chapter 5: frequently asked questions

[1]See *The Old Man Living in My Head: One Guy's Musings About the Bible* for a longer, more detailed look at how this happens.

[2]Romans 12:2

[3]See *The Fingerless Lady Living in My Head: One Guy's Musings About Tolerance* if you're still curious about how I kick certain ideas out of my head.

chapter 6: on having been given a head

[1]See *The Old Man Living in My Head: One Guy's Musings About the Bible* for more on how this has all gone down in my head.

conclusion: your head

[1]You can find the answers to these questions, and further your tour of my upstairs, by reading one of the other odd books about my head listed on the following page.

ONE GUY'S HEAD SERIES

A bunch of ideas are running around in Don Everts's head. Some are permanent residents. Others are visitors, just passing through. When they all get together, some odd things start happening.

All the Ideas Living in My Head: One Guy's Musings About Truth, ISBN: 978-0-8308-3611-6

The Old Man Living in My Head: One Guy's Musings About the Bible, ISBN: 978-0-8308-3612-3

The Dirty Beggar Living in My Head: One Guy's Musings About Evil & Hell, ISBN: 978-0-8308-3613-0

The Fingerless Lady Living in My Head: One Guy's Musings About Tolerance, ISBN: 978-0-8308-3614-7

LIKEWISE. *Go and do.*

A man comes across an ancient enemy, beaten and left for dead. He lifts the wounded man onto the back of a donkey and takes him to an inn to tend to the man's recovery. Jesus tells this story and instructs those who are listening to "go and do likewise."

Likewise books explore a compassionate, active faith lived out in real time. When we're skeptical about the status quo, Likewise books challenge us to create culture responsibly. When we're confused about who we are and what we're supposed to be doing, Likewise books help us listen for God's voice. When we're discouraged by the troubled world we've inherited, Likewise books encourage us to hold onto hope.

In this life we will face challenges that demand our response. Likewise books face those challenges with us so we can act on faith.

likewisebooks.com

DATE DUE
